THE LOOM

UNIVERSITY OF CALGARY
Press

The Loom

ANDY WEAVER

Brave & Brilliant Series
ISSN 2371-7238 (Print) ISSN 2371-7246 (Online)

University of Calgary Press
2500 University Drive NW
Calgary, Alberta
Canada T2N 1N4
press.ucalgary.ca

LIBRARY AND ARCHIVES CANADA CATALOGUING IN PUBLICATION

Title: The loom / Andy Weaver.
Names: Weaver, Andy, 1971- author
Series: Brave & brilliant series.
Description: Series statement: Brave & brilliant series | Includes bibliographical references.
Identifiers: Canadiana (print) 20240437136 | Canadiana (ebook) 20240437152 | ISBN 9781773855837 (softcover) | ISBN 9781773855820 (hardcover) | ISBN 9781773855844 (PDF) | ISBN 9781773855851 (EPUB)
Subjects: LCGFT: Poetry.
Classification: LCC PS8595.E175 L66 2024 | DDC C811/.6—dc23

The University of Calgary Press acknowledges the support of the Government of Alberta through the Alberta Media Fund for our publications. We acknowledge the financial support of the Government of Canada. We acknowledge the financial support of the Canada Council for the Arts for our publishing program.

Printed and bound in Canada by Imprimerie Gauvin
♻ This book is printed on Enviro natural paper

Editing by Helen Hajnoczky
Cover image: Juan Pedro Chabalgoity, [Man Drawing Bust], ca. 1875, photo collage, 10.5 x 6.3 cm, The Metropolitan Museum of Art, New York, https://www.metmuseum.org/art/collection/search/764772.
Cover design, page design, and typesetting by Melina Cusano

For Kelly

*Co-author of our two greatest texts
and my unshakeable ally against them,
our small but relentless opponents*

a sharp
wail

inside
the

after
noon's

quiet
shell

the grain's
art

starts the
fine

layers
of

mother
ing

pearles
cence .

When I had journeyed half my life's way,
I found I'd lost sight of love—just the sort
of line that mediocre, middle-aged men
have been using since the evolution
of male pattern baldness. But I did not
buy a convertible to follow the sun
nor an illicit houseboat on which to
float secretly away from my age
-appropriate wife and towards a
spectacular toupee.
                        But there's nothing
particularly special about half way—
don't we always feel like we're drawn in
pencil while the eraser is working
equally hard? Even worse, don't we get
used to the feeling our life is a rock
not-so-slowly chipped away each day, that
we live as debtors withdrawing hourly
from a sum owned by some other self
to whom we owe an amount constantly
on the edge of coming due?
                        O, boo-hoo!
You can shrug and say "We're fucked," or try
something new, risk buckling under the weight
of anchoring yourself inside a time
and place, becoming a fully entrenched
person in the bewildering motley
medley of musics where the abstract
and the concrete collide.
                        At such a point,
to love is a monstrous leap   of the mind,
a protest, a mouth speaking the soft substance
of a body in a language too inherent
for us to translate.
                        But we choose, fully
aware of the contradictions, to seek
a type of language that will move us
beyond the alienation. Beyond

wit's end, beyond white sound, beyond rite's
grounds, we chase blindly a restoration
between mind and matter, our words and
reality.
           This is our stubborn belief
in love's mandate, this is the difference,
the remainder, the extraneous sum
we carried home as children, alongside
the change from the corner store tucked like burning
stones inside our shoe, a heightened awareness
that the unsatisfying condition
of the present can, after all, be changed.

But sometimes you just have to shut up and
get on the roller coaster. Dear Reader,
I'm exhausted already and even
the angels don't want to wear these red shoes
in which I can't dance around the subject
any longer:

           I am terrified.

In other words, the baby is home now.
In *other* other words, in order to
understand, in order to truly stand
inside love, I want to know what it *is*
and grasp
           how
                   it sits like action in the heart
of inaction, far past description,
prescription, or performance,
                               how by day
we praise it as generous while at night
we lament our greed,
                       how, intoxicated,
it makes us sing beer songs to the little birds,
to the red birds, to the yellow birds, hell,
let's sing to all the birds, secret heroes

of evolutionary success,
                              how
sometimes it refuses our songs and,
like lead in alchemy, love confuses
our desire to reimagine it.

What *is* it?
                    I'm so scared by the question,
one which has bested both Dante and
Foreigner, Plato and Haddaway.

Baby,
            don't hurt me if I say here,
plainly, at the start, I doubt I'll find
a simple, single answer. In other words,
my only guess is that the answer cannot
be singular.
                    Or perhaps this confusion,
the exhaustion of the frenzied mêlée,
is a means of gathering different chords,
traces of new trajectories, reforming
the webs in a tangle where everything
encounters a fresh togetherness
in the gravity well of the moment?

With no form other than our buried
complexes of character, our past selves
gloriously too much, too unutterable,
too utterly unununderstandable,
we stand rebirthed on the brink, before
each other, lingering pillars covered
in forgotten hieroglyphs where we,
as readers, slide our fingers along
the chisel marks to recompose the key
of a different code and take part in
reinventing the mythology.
                              Like
a kaleidoscope's constant transformation,

like a remembered fragrance of mother's
milk on the newborn's tongue, the adept
adapt to presence, letting the virtue
of attraction pinpoint the wobbling pivot
that lets us negotiate our worlds,
knowing we'll soon enough be off-balanced
by the staggers and jags, lagging too heavy
at the mouth and heaving our tongues like great
marine mammals,
                         until we're pulled forward
with the words of love burning our lips, love
words slipped like holy ashes into parts
of ourselves we have burnished with small
delicate touches of what could otherwise
seem the lack of our simple days.
                                        So, in
my stippled ways, I love you, I pour what
I can of you into me, what I can
of me into you.
                         But then again
my simplicity misses the mark,
there is no simplex, no "my," though in
these words I find you, indelible,
and though you remain as inscrutable
in your nearness as the sequence of moles
starred on your skin which I must study
to learn my simplest self.
                                   If there is
a "me," it is surely only through
your squiggling yous that I know it, so
I'm willing to teeter on the totter
of these clichés in order to show it.

And so love is and is more than the word
and the word's purgatorial world
                                        —it
is the dance of attendance, the presence
in the present that holds us in the here,

the now, the embrace of the beloved.
The baby, like the unseen waves of time,
like gravity, as always: grasping; gasp
-ing.

    But to speak of this is not enough
faced with life's self-questioning, our self
important questing.
              The horizon recedes
as it eternally concedes. We cannot
speak of this. The words have been lifted
from our mouths, the mind mapped in its made
container, language and its mad wages. But
we cannot
        not speak.
             Your tongue burns the tips
of my words. To speak of you is the simplest
thing
    but simple through complication,
our new complicity in a complex
simplicity, a new feeling about
composition.
         Such comprehension
is something more than consumption, and so
all beloveds reveal themselves to me
as the explosion of an unknowable
wager shimmering on the cusp of
presence,
        not the fireworks in the night sky
but their visual perseveration
lingering on the eye, malingering
in the mind.
        Or, to risk speaking more
precisely, they exist as a perpetually
skimming stone, denting but never breaking
the merging of air, water, thrust, that it
never stops driving in its documenting;
less a vocabulary than an

assembling of words that structures briefly
a moment of time with no diminishment,
each of us receiving and passing to
others more and more, a stone on which
was built the tale of the loaves and the fish.

On this rock, we learn to praise by day
the generous, by night to praise the greedy.

Ah, but this is stupid stuff. Just remember
that the world, alert in its today,
the divine envelope, is the only
place where light slips through the turning leaves,
that though even sound decays through space
and we cannot speak of our truest selves,
we can agree that to think geography
alone defeats desire is a brutal
dismissal of the mind that we, a heady
species of mapmakers and road builders,
have never allowed.
                    For all our faults,
we have always chosen love; though we'll never
find the way, we refuse to believe we're lost.

Merely the littlest speech, then, not only speaks
but respeaks love into the world;
                              yes, we tend
to overlook the simplest answers, but
a hidden order shines among all things.
We worry to watch the birds flitter,
hatchling, nestling to fledgling and first
falling flight—but they trust their beautiful
feathers, more complex than the accumulation
of pearls and more complicatedly joined
than the letters of the alphabet. All there,
a purpose beyond complexity, to
fly.
      Dante, in his journey, eventually

stumbled past not only the lion,
the leopard, and the needlessly gendered
she-wolf—hell, he even fumbled his way
out of allegory and reached heaven,
the Empyrean, the metaphysical
light he knew as the clarity of his
god's love. Pretty good for a guy who
got lost walking in his walled neighborhood
in Florence.
        In my fatherhood the walls
have fallen, spring birds have returned, and I
am lost in a divine confusion, answers
swirling around us on the downy
barbs of inexplicable feathers.

～～～.

CLEAVE

(For Duncan Thomas Laycock Weaver)

I•know•of•no••evidence•love•f
osters•pure•diversity•or•kin
dness,•that•it•is•more•utopi
a•than•it•is•hell;•it•is•a•h
inge•that•flourishes•where•a
ll•ideologies'•binaries•fail
,•a•register•not•of•what•has
•happened•but•of•what•might,
•a•prehistory•of•humanity,•p
erhaps•even•humaneness,•yet•
to•come,•collected•in•symbol
s•only•initiates•can•read.•B
ut•there•are•no•initiates.•S
o•we•cannot•trust,•of•all•pe
ople,•the•lovers•to•understa
nd•the•forces•of•love•that•r
emind•us•mathematics•is•more
•metaphor•than•truth,•as•the
•thought•separating•one•from
•two•is•nothing•compared•to•
that•between•nothing•and•one
.•We•cannot•let•ourselves•th
ink•of•the•form•of•the•thing
•as•the•container•of•the•thi
ng•contained,•for•the•calcul
us•of•pleasure•is•deeply•com
plex.•It•cuts.•It•splices.•I
t•multiplies.•And•it•divides

O

Here
again
writing
of what
remains

unwritten not
a narrative

A collection
of strands
strung around
their *and*s

So

Every "real"
story Every
string a lure

Contra
diction

To try
to know
to speak
but not

to stand
under

O.o

It was a dark and stormy night.
                              Unknown
sounds crept through every corner of the house.
On the dreary shelves, tomes titled *Lovecraft* and
M. R. James pulsed just out of sight, gold spines
flickering in candlelight dancing where there wasn't
a draft.

          Working subtly as a spider, the strands of your
cobweb appeared to us too late.
                              We were caught,
though I suspect but cannot prove the journey
from comfortable DINKs to trapped parents
was made by more matter than a creature
of so little weight.
                    I suppose your slender silks
must have confused our vision of this life revision
as, with a haphazard spin, we stepped in
to what we recognized only after was your
webwalker's perplexing home.
                              We sprawled,
immobilized by new fears that pumped like
a paralytic through us.
                    Or perhaps—with these
night terrors it is hard to remember now—
we were minding our mothy business,
quietly tracking moonphases, when a porch light
strategically placed behind your maze
drew us in.
          Regardless, when with unexpected
kindness you turned us loose, we ran to get help,
sure that we were free to do what we learned
afterwards was your
                    terrible bidding all along.
We brought back others, more energy for you to

feed on. But a fool's errands are still errands
to the fool, so send us on your way, spidergod,
we will walk among the unsuspecting while hidden
chords most canny and uncanny remake
my hollow chest in the shape of your homuncular
form, mirroring what is swelling

                      like a new horror
in the alembic of my wife's body

                        as it gives itself
over to yet another new organizing structure,
a second eldritch god we will learn to serve, muttering
I am not fit to judge this pure light, this dark sun
I hold, nor what it starts, in me, to ignite.

O.oo

Obvious but a point worth making:
the story of the love of division
is not the story of a division of love.

Rather,
overcome and overturned,
oblivious, flames lacking
moths, we become novels of love
in the time of syllabaries.

We linger.
We delay.
We wobble and sway.

A long syllable consists of two,
and then a short syllable consists of one.

We right the divisible in visible ink.

O.ooo

We find certain trades
inherently puzzling

because we don't find
love's whole career
puzzling enough,
                    which
is a way of saying that
the work doesn't belong
to the world
                    but rather
is itself a limit of the world,

which becomes an assay
of swaying
                    where a wife
with child is a giddiness
of definition
                    best left to
ethicists and echolocation,
a change to will that changes
unchangeably,
                    a jigsawed puzzle
of pieces illustrating a moveable
feast;
          it's neoliberalism's
worst nightmare and perhaps
its only salvation,
                    a wife *and*
a child, not yet
                    a child and a wife,
a conundrum eventually pushed
through a mystery, wrapped inside
a burgeoning newness,
                    a reimagining

where the non-sight is the sign
of the absent site.
                  Such a ward
is hard to put into words.

O.oooo

At first, it's hard to see how this division
you surrender to
                              is a precious reward—scribed
and described, languaged, defined and refined
—still surrender retains the precocious award.

In the diorama, the word is the octopus lying
in its camouflage, and the idea is the shark, ever
circling. One will devour the other, though bets
are still being taken.
                              So don't trust poetry, but
mostly ignore the insurers and their actuarial
fables. Combine the two, and we can say with
certainty that Tennessee is not blessed with hills
littered with abandoned pottery; Wallace did not
callous his executive hands depositing around
unneeded Memphian jars.
                              Symbolism and metaphor
only take us so far—the evacuation as such perfection
undoes time and the actual animality of the human.

Instead, one wonders at the sun, how it still lavishly
stuns and slavishly, endlessly overruns;
                              can we compare
this to what it means to hold a novelty like a babe in arms
and start to un-clan and re-clan, to remould ourselves,
unclad and uncanny, much like the beautiful kelly
-green grass is pulled back to expose the clay
for brickmaking, the foundation that this work
entrenches in the world?
                              A child is born and we
are borne back ceaselessly into this repast,
two starving outcasts standing in front
of the welcoming banquet, left open
-mouthed, flabbergast.

~~~

I.i

Presocratic philosophers, acutely aware
that writing only faintly
                              reproduces
the blazing intensity of an occurrence,
                                          sang
that a man who is dying,
                              shot by an arrow,
will scream the words of love
                              like sharpened shafts,
as bolts,
              wanting to wound the air,
                                          and so love
is the tongue that parts
                              the lips—pushing its way
as carelessly as the arrow
                              pierces the skin of the heart....

Ah, there's the old bullshit, the masculinist driving
its willy nilly through everything standing
in its way. Such a poor, old, tired, sawhorse.
Love is not a piercing missile, a hacking cleaver.
It does not part.
              Look closely.
                              Love never was
the arrow, it was the red blood rushing
to the wound, working from the instant
its instant pull together, a tapestry of cleaved,
of the asunder, of the parted. It's that under
which we lulled and weaved, it's the warp
and the weft, the balm of the reft, the uncleft.

It's the centripetal force, the only tether. And so
this turn undoes the fling apart, it keeps
the atoms twirling, the molecules whirling,
the fingerprints whorling, the suns burning,

the galaxies churning. No wonder, then,
that it sends our senses reeling like a spinning
bobbin as the shuttle slides through the strings
so exactly unlike the arrow's fletched nock.

I.ii

The newborn's cry soars, unlike music,
in the immaterial, an economy
without exchange where repetition
is not marginal but prophetic,
at the edge of our worldly encounters,
testing the broadest ranges of affinity:

beyond statecraft,
                            beyond five-year plans
and the invisible hand
                            of the market,
beyond the double game
                            of reproducer
and prophet,
                    beyond words of power
and words
            of subversion,
                                this divination
of sublime
                interconnection,
                                a simple
psalter of the world,
                        stretching through
all directions
                    at once.

I.iii

Still, sometimes
                    we hunt
          with the pack
we find,
sometimes
             the pack
                    destroys us.
To say it
         another way,
                      if love
        were a country,
its flag
        would be the purest
               white,
      universal colour
of surrender.
To say it
        again,
                there is
        a difference
between those
             who serve
         the system
    and those who
serve the people.
                Or to say it
for never
        the last time,
                    there are those
          we live among
     and to love them
is to free ourselves.

~~~

Incomplete, perfectly, the baby
                              launches
each sound
            as an impression
                              that is at once
modified
            and launched again,
                              second thoughts
growing out
            of initial misapprehensions,
mental actions
            reflected
                        in the soundings
and reachings
            of the syllables
                        that stretch
            for each other
      even
      as it becomes clearer and clearer
that the grasping
            will not succeed,
                              like
a bee
      -keeper's hands
                        stretched empty
in midair
            toward,
                  for,
                        in quest of,
                              after.
Sweet honey
            and infinite hunger,
the taste
            almost on the tongue,
                        your tiny,

                                taut
attention
                to the matter
                                of boundaries,
                                the flesh
                between the you
and the me.

                Probing these
                                swarming
                activations and
appropriations, the self
                                forms
                                at the buzzing edge
                        of the colony's *I*
                        before
                        the infant can learn
                        to love the absurd there-ness
                of the world, that
                                        close-at-hand
that seems
                        to baffle every entry
                                        into it.
So there you sit,
a baby with your hand
                                in the honeypot,
encountering the sweetness
                        of an impossible
                        fusion,
                        the crisis
                        of viscous contact,
                        a labile sweetling,
                        a small compilation
                of constant revisions.

                        ∼∼∼

II.i

A leafless bough, the smallest twig,
                              , drops
into the abandoned
                        workings of a salt mine.
Season after season
                        the stick crystallizes,
until it is mottled
                        with a galaxy
                                    of scintillating
                  diamonds,
                              the original wood
no longer measurable.

                              Somehow the imagination
also remakes
                        and mutates the world
around the clasp and staple
                                    of the newly
                  delivered,
            and the person reborn
as *father*
            reaches out
                              to something
                  glorious
            that recedes
at the edge of a presence.

Mother stands on the strand
                                    and stretches
                  across
                              towards the boundary
            of another.

Dazed, dazzled, we try to feel
                              this thinking,

                        to think
            this feeling,
                        and we drive
                        ourselves
onto a blind spot
                in the self
where our gaze
                disappears from us
in the act
            of gazing
                    at
                    a truly new
                    newness.

We try to walk
                on this ledge
                that brings only
                a fall
                into vertigo,
a spin of ecstasy
                    where there is no stillness,
a point where we can
                    no longer peacefully
converge
            like king or queen
                            into one state,
                            one noun,
                            the place
where we see there was
never such a thing as original,
only a series
            of origins
                        played
                        out as
                this squirming
                shoreline
between actual
                and possible.

≈≈≈

II.ii

An overflowing river
is a threat and a source
of bounty, so every
government eventually
gets the same brilliant
plan, buys sandbags and
declares *We'll bend this raging*
torrent to our purposes
or drown trying while old
-timers in the flood zone
cackle, stock up on wellingtons
and hip waders, check
the firmness of the house's
foundations.
                Love works
in a similar system
of exchanges,
a swelling danger
that can easily wash
away the unprepared.
We live to learn under
the mercy of this
generalized threat.

And yet this toddler
is no passive mirror
to the power of his time:
while the waters rise,
he, a timid deer, steps,
stops, and stays, a bestiary
of bestill, seemingly
motionless and almost
deadened by the powering
flow until, like that wild
woodland creature,

he always eventually
squats, dribbles, and high
steps along on his relieved
way.
    Sure, authority will try
to stem or aim the river's path,
but, like in movies where
the heatwave brings with it
a tampered inner-city hydrant,
streams will always scatter
wherever they want, among
the shouts and roars of laughter
because a strange joy for all
exists in this randomized lottery
of removing the boy's diaper.

Simple joys for this besotted
man.
    In other words, though
the watercannon is strong enough
to worry our eyes, compared
to such moments of lawless,
squealing refreshment, the forces of order
are just pissing in the wind.

∾∾∾

II.iii

At least, that's all this weaving
has taught me.
           If it seems, child,
your hands are quite small, take it
from me, they are not. The wheel
is not. The world is not. Love is not
—and yet when it needs to be, it is,
and so are you, my tiny lockpick.

But none of us is too pure or too
tarnished for this life, even Villon
plundered and murdered before
writing his perfect poems, and,
my little thief, I see you take
in everything like you're stealing
gold coins from the church, ready
to sew them into the linings
of your plush pampers like
you've been banished by the king
to wander throughout the rainy season,
then, granted pardon, you disperse
all your cares and joys carelessly
like all good balladeers.
                 And, yes,
I can be as maudlin as the next
three guys, but sometimes
we must get down to efficacy—
so never mind the snows, Duncan,
in December we must ask where
are the shovels of yesteryear.

III.i

Fluttering little somniphobe,
every moment flits away from you
and your proper response to flight
is fight. This is the hummingbird's
flying tune, an ancient rite, a droning
delight refusing to admit the day's fuse
burns into the night.
                              My indefatigable
seagull, my young skittery pigeon,
my winter's goldfinch flittering
a centre to the world's ceaseless
and boring dissolution, my cogito
nicely summed, my you, my yous,
·my goose-quill source delicately shaped
and hewn.
                    Like you, I can only speculate
on the effect that a day's proper seed caching
might have had on the night's comfort,
but to talk of sleep, unaccustomed
as we are to risking the window's threshold
of the legible, is to try to stare into
a voided notverse that blinks in the corner
of all our vision, a notion in motion
curled around every moment of stasis.

A love, like sleep, that doesn't aspire
to some degree of illegibility would be
a hawkish nightmare.
                              Reflected in this
little merlin's eye I view sleep's battle,
the self caught in the thermal's unpunctual
moment as it pushes your wings upward
and away again and again from the nest's
downy rest, as you catch the sun's surprise
each time and eagle eye the world

into itself, see all this sleepy carnality
just in time to catch how the ancient glass
distorts the transparent window. Another
near miss as you go careening away.
                                    This
wild eye prisms my day, distorts the
setting sunlight until through you I see
a refracted world, a globe where even
time's light seems to bend to the burning
immolation of your phoenix-like glow.

III.ii

Could the world of divine things
ever correspond to the baby's passion
for a shifting sea of forms in which
self and other forge a union where
milk, not death, is the extreme limit
of experience?
        This is too difficult
for my masculinist thought, just as
the occult symbology of alchemy
is inconsistent and deliberately
recalcitrant—
        such magic's ancient
premise is that when like calls to like
there's a need to conceal the processes
from the uninitiated, those who haven't
learned that the immanence of the cosmos
lies wholly in the least significant, the least
signifying, of its parts.
        Still, the words
for love are just strivings for a shared
devotion, weak denials of the distancing
that belies the clarity we seek to give
ourselves.
        The mirrors we hold
continuously warp clear sense into
distortion, the discovery that love
ceaselessly triggers: transparency
is incompatible with the temporal
nature of temptation, a distraction
from the actual.
        So the outline of your
little hand traced onto paper tells us
more about the weariness of graphite
than about the damp heat of your grasp
—experience exists always already

outside and beyond, and the poets
most of all recognize that hell is this
sliding back down the sentences
they tried to use to climb out of it,
the weight of the words breaking
the linkages as they form them.

III.iii

Yet language is
the only song we have,
and so there is a sort
of heroism in how
we inhabit it
awkwardly, ghosts
newly made flesh.

I walk down the street
and sing "Blackbird,"
your strong little hands
in mine; playing puppet,
your arms dangle like
tiny wires from mine
as you swing and jump
over the sidewalk's cracks.
Your mother's back, you
say, is safe for another day.
I can only gawk and marvel
at the blue fairy's work.

Despite the charlatanry
and sophistry, the summer
is summer, the spring rabbits
are growing and healthy and faster
than the dogs, the nuthatches
still find the feeder. Say what
you will how you will, we all
always wait for this moment
to arise. A song leaves your lips
and pulls everything in sight
towards baptism.

∿∿∿

III.iv

Perhaps if a new content is
a new devotion, the result
of novel imagination, then
there is love even in reason—if
emotion is the first evolution
making ways for new forms of life,
then love is what gives us reason
for reason and saves us from the crushing
reality of reality.
                        But such theories
imply the result reveals its system
and overlook the estrangement
within replication in order to install us
within a tradition where the structure
results from the base,
                        Christ,
                                    the horror
of baby is
                as daddy done does.

Could love ever exist without the lovers'
imperfections, each action that
recreates, reimagines, re-embodies
vague ideas into actualities,
a new, never-ending series of
annunciations of our lord and lady,
manifested (womanifested? babyfested?)
within us all?
                So when I hold you,
I re-form love, when I read to you
I revise love, when your arms hold me
at night as I put you to bed I am
re-molded by exacted, factual love.

∽∽∽

IV.i

You are learning
to walk as awk
wardly as though
you carry an un
seen empty and
unwieldy bask
et brimming
with not-yets
possibilities
of futures filled
with yet-to-comes

Still you step
and I see never
ending falling be
fore us all
        So every
moment we mumble
not-yet not
yet and we under
stand we cultivate
and we endure
death only as
a possibility
we understand not
as we stare at
a meaning but
as the experience
of the impossible
possibility of
impossibility
an unscalable
invisible mountain
in front of every
step

         Still
you step
and my body's
gestetner beats out
the copies each
moment whole
tracts of falling
into unsup
portable
loss nearing
forever the end
of its run
              But why
lament the actual
for destroying
mere potentials

It is
what it
is and
though
I do not
see how
this song
could possibly
be an elegy
              your stamping is
              so strong each
              careening step
but every
elegy begins
in the face
of a small
race of
destructions
downfalling
there all along

So as we all
come to see
to love
is to start
the elegy

IV.ii

And so, when we speak of death
perhaps we always also speak of love,
perhaps that's when it's most palpable,
when the elastic is stretched furthest
and cuts into our fingers. And instinct
holds on tightest when something tries
to pull it away, we think of grip, tendons,
fatigue. Or how we notice our mouth most
when the wasp threatens to enter it—not
a honey bee, with its Southern Gentleman,
Foghorn Leghorn façade of manners,
Sahr, Ah would nevah—I say nevah—
sting you, upon mah honour, for
Ah could nevah then retrieve
mah barbed stingah from your person
and so would surely visit upon mahself
a much greatah hahm than evah
would Ah bestow upon you—no,
not the bee but the wasp enters
our mouth and swells our tongue,
the words are stoppered and
caught in our throats, yet still
we speak of love. We cannot not.

The pain is too great, and yet.

The loss is too great, and yet.

The void is too great, and yet.

Priscila, whom I hardly know,
lies dying several dozen miles away,
mourned greatly by some I love.
Sometimes the transitive principle
does hold, and so I mourn, for both

the mourned and the mourning,
and love holds, stretches and holds
as a mediation between banquet
and austerity, our attempt to make
the alienation of life bearable
through a prolonged partaking
of the communion of grief,
a space between fear and food
that contracts our lives in a shared
misunderstanding of the size of the world,
a way of speaking of the world in words
that bind it in our common reality.

IV.iii

And all the while, love keeps churning
our yearning, its beguiling lure gyring
always just out of reach, until the austringer
mans the hawk. Though we bite and bate,
the jesses and creance will hold.

Try as we might, we are not our own,
others describe our circles, others
classify, define, taxonomize our meanings.

Love reminds us that we hold within us
neither meaning nor finality, though we fight
to assign signification to certain sounds
and actions with the haughty indifference
associated with ancient heraldry
or the forgotten art of the soothsayers
who read what was written in the entrails
of birds. We're left to learn and relearn
the anticipation that's a source of excessive pain.

Operating in the theatre of life, our interplay
of growths and amputations, double-edged love
is both integrator and subverter, a ladder
that connects the rungs even as it holds them
apart forever. If noise carries each possible
meaning within itself;
                            if corruption
is the revelation of purity;
                            if we grieve
at the sight of life passing through death's sieve
—what's borne is not born without crisis,
transcending the old violences and biases
to make new systems of violence, of bias, of boundary.

A mutation, a catastrophe, a continuation, love
ceaselessly transcribes, ascribes, and proscribes
as it spins new orders into the very kingdoms
and phyla of love.

V.i

Whatever love is, it surely is not
a philosophy but—like philosophy—
a belief in a world that can be bettered
that binds us all but isn't provable
beyond the small share we each carry,
a key, a knife, a piece of melting ice
that burns us because we don't dare let it
go as it drips away, an everlasting
remainder of what is left us and left
beyond us.
         And so, in the end, we must
admit that love does cleave after all,
it ceaselessly cleaves, in all senses
of the word, all at once rendering asunder
and holding together, letting us see
what we are and what we lack, a glimpse
of the impossible mechanics
of time, as old loves still make claims on us
and we move forward by going back
to honour them. So confusion is our core,
profusion is our principle, and
exclusion is our undoing.
              Your little
outline moves on the wall and we note it
without ever knowing the shadow—so,
troubled that the Oracle at Delphi
proclaimed him the wisest of men, Socrates
lived his life plagued by the question *can
the difference between what is known and what
is unknown truly be wisdom*, which he
couldn't answer because he loved the difference
too dearly.
         Still, through each attachment there is
a single fear, a feeling that no one will
ever whisper to us our truest name.

Yet, when there is an elegant solution,
aesthetics excels at finding it,
and the positions your hands sign into
the air, your grasping reaches and flailings,
are the theories we need to see there is nothing
there, there is no *there*, only constellations
of here, you dispute any argument
for profound loneliness, you argue that
true solitude is an orderliness
completely alien to life.
                      Wrapped like
an ancient Greek in your blanket, you orate,
you profess and expound that love in all
its manifestations is never obvious,
and that to exaggerate its features
for something as alien as clarity
is to ruin the artistry of the
actual and the manifold intricacies
of its interlacing iterations.

<p style="text-align:center">~~~</p>

V.ii

And so this is where we live,
on the shocking border
of the plurality of the singular self,
sometimes alone and yet never outside
the sweeping register of the dance,
of accumulation, a grand numberless
collection continuing the grand conversation,
the eternal dissensus of people
encountering people, the world,
the thought of the thought held
in a space of interview, the dream
of a shared language, of the loosing
of bounds through the commingling of bonds,
this absurd Esperanto we name as love.

V.iii

Still, over and over we turn
and return to the pages
of the book, as though these
bound leavings were a site
of love,
       but it would be better
to speak of some grand, never
-ending '70s ouroboric rolodex
overfilled with an overflow of addresses

—and so let the glitter balls drop,
pull the rhinestone jumpsuits
and bellbottoms out of storage
because you should slide
electrically through this
boogie wonderland, you
dancing queens and kings,
for it is an undeniable truth
that you can't write of discovery
without disco.
        And because of you,
for you, I am crazy like a fool, I play
Daddy Cool over and again and
break out my white man's overbite
and you dance, your mother dances
so your *in utero* brother dances, and we all
dance together precisely because we know
someone *is* watching,
           we scream
and laugh because what is noise
to the old order is harmony to the new.
The instrument pre-dates the music
it allows, breaking through the old
talk of death, sin, and taxes
to renew the syntax.

<div align="center">~~~</div>

V.iv

Love trapped in a single identity, then,
dissolves and dissipates by hardening
into itself, the tree bough crystallizes
in the salt mine until it is brittle as dust,
suppleness sacrificed in the name of fixity.
Many will ask if Lent must supplant
Carnival for the Round to eventually re-
emerge.
      But there is no safe love, we must
bargain for it at the crossroads, ceaselessly
reinvent new pathways into and through
the world. There is neo-love or there is
naught.
      Philosophers say what is essential
in thought is what we cannot say—so
the future of love is not its existence
but our lack, our suffering, our trouble,
and we return again to the crisis now,
forever, in process, and we cleave together
as we cleave apart, a piece of the apparatus
tasked with speaking the glory of the fulcrum,
as even Bach was contracted to a Count, his hymns
placed in a position of servility
                  —and all
the while, somewhere, there is a black hole,
from which nothing escapes, a darkness invisible,
predatory, the proof of which science looks for
out there
      when all the time it sits at the end
of speech, of listening, of musical phrase,
all trapped within a common type of sentence.

So, at times, we dare the new, and love leads us
forward like a bird of fire, immolating us all,
destroying what we are, and setting free

those few seeds that need to burn to kindle
into life;
    other times, in the name of safety,
we slip into a comfort that softens the soul
of the revolution as we settle for the familiar
wrongs we've known all along.
         Duncan,
I cannot lie and tell you which is better,
or if a better exists—but I can say a change
in the nature of love changes the code, that
a language must contain both variance and unity,
an impossible politics that demands we walk
the awkward cusp of every meeting point,
that we recognize the voids between us
while we talk and reach over those gaps.

It would be easy to say that the present
—already built around the ideas of walls
and borders, the bluster and lies of separation,
a time when it feels impossible to find
the foundations and fundamentals—
it's easy to say that this will change,
but I don't know it will change for the better.

So my every desire is defeated and yet
still desires. What I know is that you
are here and that I love you, that you
will change and I will love you, that you
will desire, defeat, surrender, and I
will love you. Just so. You are fact.

ligament
       /
             ligature

I stand
        at the pivot point
                        balanced
like an open
            book
                    tented
on its wobbling
                covers,
                        spine miraculously
but barely
            holding
                    it all together.

This is
        the zenith, the crest
                            in the wave.

Forty-five
            behind
                    and the same
before,
        I imagine, since
                        years are just
fancies of our
                dizzied
                        twirlings, nothing .
more.

        Or less. Today
                        there is no less,
and what
            could seem
                        from such a peak
a certain
            lessening
                        is rather

a readiness,
        like a car
            in a roller
coaster
       at the very
            tip
before
      the plunge,
           filled
with prospects
        of glee
           and catalyzing
fears
     that hold
        no real fear—
at the bottom
        another climb
           will begin,
just
   one
     I
cannot see
       from the heights
          that dazzle
me now.

When I
     was younger, I
          expected love
to be
    the answer
       to the secret
that, like a living
       fossil,
         a coelacanth,
was never hidden
      just

                    unconcerned
with anyone
          who didn't
                    search deeply for it
—a thought
          so convoluted
                    it's still impossible
to parse
     if I thought
               I was seeking
out the answer
          or the secret.
                    Or maybe
we learn
     to cherish
          the moments
of boredom
          as necessary
                    parts
of the game,
          and so,
               if nothing else,
the search
     eventually grounded out
                         to first
by bunting away
          the awful
               stodgy seriousness
of the serious
          young man
               or at least
popped out
     a forgetfulness
               of the mercenary
unkindness
          of my swings
               at "true love,"
the bedevilments

of so much
unwanted adoration
and the paltry
concerns
of the innermost
enchantments
of a mind
so self
revolved.
Eventually
I learned
to manage,
to see
the home stand
can only
be
salvaged
by a series
of intentional
sacrifices.

Yet a part
of us
always dreads
that type of success,
distrusts
anything difficult
as artificial.
We all want
to be
the slightly roughened
and tarnished
Redford
rounding the bases
while crowds cheer out
proof
we were right
to never settle

                        to never give in
to what we
            think
                    are the world's
unfair tricks,
                a series
                        of threats and bribes.
Then,
        suddenly,
                    we're
the old men
            and that dirty money
                            looks awful
clean against
                what we've already
                            mortgaged.

But maybe love
                is actually
                            the harm
and the solace,
                all that
                        which cuts us
open
        to the world,
                    what pitches us
away
        and toward,
                    we are constantly
thrown
        by it,
                knuckling
our way
        toward the glove,
                        the ground,
the bat,
            never
                knowing

where
            we're headed,
                            only realizing that
the arc
            of the pitcher's arm
                                    mirrors
the galaxy's
            swirl,
                        that through
its parts
            the universe
                        posits
a sum
            and the silliness of games
                                    ends.

But we learn
            different games
                                    always
begin,
            it's how we teach,
                        and so
the rabbit
            must circle
                        and dive
through its hole,
                your little fingers
                                    must grab
this potential
                that drives your most
                                    incurable wants,
continually
            vanishing, always over
                                    there.
The shoe
            will not
                        stay tied,

the knot

     will not

          knot but

that does not

        mean that

            an untie,

a terrible naught

         that unbinds,

               should be taught

as an answer

       to shield you

            from feeling distraught.

Give in

     to velcro?

        As you joke,

a frayed knot.

       And so,

          as people

have always done,

       you trip

         and fall

and fall

    again,

      all,

all because

     the fall

        is the art

of your innermost

       self, twisting in

           upon itself

as it folds

      others into

        its tangle.

There is

    no real language

         for the fear

in this submission,

      yet a desire

                              to be submerged
is the learned practice
                    and event
                              in and of
the beloved
              —the cycle
                    has no resolution,
no force
            of conclusion,
                          because the risk
of submergence
                    around another
                                is the first
endless
          task,
                  though it becomes
so snarled
            you sometimes
                          lose
contact
          with the materiality
                              that grounded
you
      as a single strand
                      at the start,
and you feel
              betrayed,
                          like you are
angry love
            trapped in the hands
                                of a sinful god.

And so
        we attend,
                    we learn
to attend,
            pushing

                        past
mere
        perception
                        as we callous
our knees
                while we tend
                                to the moment
of our bodies
                in the world.
                                Coercion,
I agree,
        is the only
                        true evil,
but listen
                to the alacritous
                                world
with alacrity
                and doubt
                        every slack-jaw,
all the lockjaws'
                        talk of lack,
                                The world
dwindles,
                they say,
                        when I can tell you
actually that
                the world
                        so lessons
us in wonder
                even our words
                                whirl.
There is
        no
                lessening,
though
        the little
                *ubi-sunt*ers
will always

                    wait
                            in the corridors
lamentatiously
                    lamenting
                            the lamentable
mutability
            of lamented things,
                                the transitions
of life,
            the losses
                        they've learned
to clutch
            to, and so
                        they mourn
the caterpillars,
                    the robins'
                            blue eggs.
Sag,
        they preach,
                        because the world
tumbles
        and flags.

But Pink
            Floyd
                    be damned,
science
            and even the smug
                                little poetasters
know
        there is
                    no dark
side
        to the moon.
                        Eclipses
constantly black out
                        planets

                    throughout
the universe,
              but they don't
                        make the universe
any darker.
          And perhaps
                    the sun
won't always rise.
                Perhaps.
                    Or perhaps it's
that the idea
          of setting
                    is only a trick
of perspective
          to begin with.
                    Perhaps.
Or perhaps,
          you will find,
                    opinions
are like butt plugs
              —some people
                        will try
to shove them
          up your
                    aspects of understanding.
Kansas,
        I don't think
                  we're *in toto* anymore
—but the sun
          remains,
                    and remains for
the shadowed
          a simple
                    step
to one side
          or the other.
                    The system
works

but perhaps
only for the systemic
and so
we say
the lover works
without
—not
a plan,
but
without the structure
of limitations:
the writer
works
from one side
of the page
to the other,
the painter builds
layer
upon layer
from the canvas
out,
the sculptor works
outside
in
but the lover's
work is
ineffable,
perhaps
it is
the unutterable
it
self.

The equation,
such as it is,
is not
helpful:
a runner

                        by running,
a swimmer
                by swimming—
                                but
a lover
            is never made
                            just by loving,
the necessity
                of a beloved
                                makes love
unique.

            *   *   *

Days later,
            I can add
                        only
that while
            we are creatures
                            rented
like mules
            by obsession
                            for the collection
of moments,
                shoring up
                            each fragment
as a rampart
                against our
                            ruinations,
no one
            wants love
                        for a time,
we want it
                forever,
                            for all time,
in a time
                that is outside
                            of time.

Fallacious logic,
            to be sure,
                        but who
questions
            precisely
                        how
love
        persuades us
                    of its
insights,
            how at times
                        it drives us
to outstrip
            ourselves
                        into betterment,
shows us all
            to be
                        equal
parts
        hero,
                minotaur,
and labyrinth.
                A gadfly
                            sent
to disturb us
            from our dozy
                        state,
love harries
            us
                until we flow
like water
            sliding
                        along wool
from fuller
            cup
                to emptier
and,
        parched slaves,

                          we start
drinking now,
                    always now,
                                whether
we're brimming
                  or nearly drained.
                                      While the body
of every
              creature,
                            every plant,
every molecule
                    and atom
                                on earth
is pervaded
                  by attraction,
                                  where there is
dissimilarity
                  between things
                                  there is also
difference between
                      what they
                                  adore
and how
        —so the soil
                        loves rain,
the sky
          loves the rain,
                            but not as the flower
loves rain,
              nor how it loves
                                  the sun.
The string we cross
                      holds tension
                                      but not
as the guitar does,
                      the note
                                is not
a transitive

property.
There is no
passing over,
there is only
what is,
what remains,
and what communion
with the world
requires of it
—that is how
life alters
and how
it altars.
Even language
evolves
as love
convolves,
atoms stumbling
into the great
tumble,
a file
of life,
filiations
and striations
of the living,
each particle
a receptacle
of an ecstatic
whole
we experience
whorled
and twined
in the warp
and weft,
a cleft
folded
in on itself,
the world's instrument

unseen,
      unsung,
            strung in
plain sight,
       a single lyre
               pulsing
with the systole
         and diastole
               of the song,
the first wage
       we earn.

Yesterday,
      in the backyard,
               the dog
surprised
      a squirrel
            completely clouded
by autumnal
       demands, Briggs
             chasing it
back and forth
       in smaller zigs
             and zags until
the squirrel
      finally
          maneuvered
a crucial
      mistake
        into a slip
under the fence.
        Throughout,
            it did not
drop
    its acorn.
        This, perhaps,
is the emblem

        of love
                —or perhaps
the dog's
        incessant drive
                is an equal
example.
        Perhaps both
                serve better
as metaphors
        for reference
                itself
—but what is
        love
            if not reference,
cobbling
        scraps of words,
                processes
of accretion
        then syncretion,
                usury,
creation *ex*
        nihilo.
            Homophones,
homonyms,
        synonyms,
                words placed
at the feet
        of another,
                not as offerings
on an altar
        —more
            scampering pups,
the only worship
        we have,
                language, after all,
as game.
        Old Ammons,
            hitting his head

on the nail:
            if love were likely
                        it would not be
love. Or,
            to adjust Olson,
                        who likely
cribbed Confucius,
                        nothing
                                    is sayable
without saying
                        it (which
                                    is not to say
it's inevitable).
                        And still the said
                                    is unsaid
to each person
                        who hasn't
                                    heard it.

Beloveds,
            yours
                        are the names
spun
        into each
                        strand
of the web
                flexing in the wind
                                    like a lung,
taut
        and slack,
                        every lock
and band
                platted
                        and plaited.
We revolve
                the senses
                            with one
another

                    into the heart
                                of all matter,
and our
            best explanation
                                    if we're forced
to spell
            it out
                        is the flexibility
in the complexity
                        of the loops
                                    and tethers
where the whole
                    of things
                                learns
to flow
            together-apart
                            toward a shimmering,
receding
            horizon,
                        nomad within monad,
and so
            we contain
                        not just multitudes
but mazes,
            folds upon fold,
                                these twisted
paths,
        as we pick
                    through the aftermath
that is love,
            our loves,
                        our loves'
love
        for us.
                    This perpetual
attendance
                breaks
                        the abundance

free
      of prediction,
                  or we
are left
      with an empty
                  language
of empty forms.

But, yes,
      to read
            the news
is to be
      reminded
            of the seeming
imperviousness
            of the world
                  to improvement.
We shake
      our heads
            and say
the political
      is not inherent
                  in love
nor in the
      good intentions
                  of its use.
Just as easy
      to say a plot
                  is where
stories
      are placed
            after they die.
But whether
      we are glib
                  or not,
things will always
            fit

                        together,
it's the undeniable
                    principle
                            of magic:
two
        inconsequential
                        things fuse,
through
            confluence
                        and confusion,
they combine
                to birth
                        a consequence
—so a person,
                a thing,
                        is never
to be judged
                alone,
                        it is never
itself
        alone,
                there's no detaching
from
        the crazy
                roundabout,
the swirling
                of the wording
                        and its many
worldings.
            Love,
                    in other words,
is other words,
                ligament,
                        ligature,
always in
            the joining
                    force
that pulls

together
the row of dots
until they
align,
an incitement
that verbs
the noun.

Accuracy, I've read,
is not
the voice of nature.
Nor is it,
I'd suggest,
one of the tongues
of love,
and so we speak
generally
not of knowing
love but
of making it,
we
are part
of the encounter,
a point
of transition
in a wobbling pivot
that spins
its necessary
precession,
and our writing
represents it,
not
in the written,
but in
the metonym
of the pen's point
on paper,
the site itself,

                         lost
in the moment
              of the scribble,
                             an occurrence
actioning
         its madcap
                    coherence
of actualizing
              and actualness.
                             So neither
the hourglass
             nor the spilling
                             sand
are in any way
              time
                   and yet
are slipped
           completely
                      inside it
—the godpage
            on which
                     the godtext
forms
     the beloved's eye,
                       a demanding
of long
       and close
                 observation,
bound
     to the infinite
                    play
of the insatiability
                    of the brevity
                                   of experience,
love is
       purely theological,
                          a supremity
whose true name

                    we dare
                              not write,
and it evolves
                    with no end point,
                                   no summation,
no synopsis.
                    It does not
                              resolve.
Perhaps I
           can only
                    explain this
by saying that,
                    while love
                              is in no way
to be confused
                    with its struggles,
                                   to lift love
out of
        the struggle
                    would be
to betray
           the struggling.

∽∽∽

THE BRIDGE

(For Hugh Nowlan Laycock Weaver)

As•abstraction,•a•bridge•e
xists•as•a•model•where•one
•element•represents•anothe
r•as•**though**•**they**•had•an•ex
changeable•value,•as•**repre**
sentation•implies•commensu
rability.•So•if•our•words•
seem•inevit**able**•it•is•beca
use•ite**ration**•limits•the•p
ast's•possibility•to•only•
the•actual,•as•you•**two**•are
•who•you•are,•**sons•and**•bro
thers,•**Kelly**'s•sons,•my•so
ns,•our•sons,•**and•always**•n
one•of•this•nonsense•**out**si
de•**of**•the•I•that•is•you•th
rough•the•we•of•this•us,•w
hatever•that•is.•So•we•sta
rted•**there**•and•we•end•here
,•we•arrive•at•the•end•of•
the•bridge•and•so•**the**•brid
ge•ceases•for•us,•takes•on
•the•presence•of•**me**mory•be
hind•actual•sensation,•the
•quick•synaptical•absence•
of•thought's•thought,•love

72

I.i

We try
      to live in the present, but

—lazy echolocations of a hazy past—

we can't make time answer
               to our needs,
our colonizing aspirations
              for a stockpile
of hours we can buttress
          and bastion
against the predations
          and dispersions
of memory's trick,
        narrative,
            the series
of cardboard cutouts
        we hold
in our mind, all we'll ever
have ever again
        of what we whisper
to ourselves
      we once had.
           We turn
to the history books, return for
their orderly mythology
        of causality,
learn to tell ourselves
          Once upon a time
the phonautograph and the paleophone
failed less
      through design
         than by a lack
of Victorian desire
      to talk to the future.

So if I argue
            we're mistaken
when we give
            more power
                        to those who record
the song
            than to the singer,
                        it doesn't mean
I don't want your love,
                        little one,
            as I spin
with you right
            round, baby,
kept safe like a record,
                        baby, right round,
round round,
            that I can turn to and play
over
            and over again.
                        Still, in an economy
built on reproduction
                        even desire becomes
a fungible object.
                        Video, then, didn't so much kill
the radio stars
            as repeat them into unstable
simulacra of life.
                        Dead or alive? Radio ga ga,
my little one,
            as you scatter your
caterwauling skittery
                        pidgin, you're *a
cappella* recitals
                        of sibilants and plosives,
your small fist
            drumming into my chest,
a one-man band
            playing out the time

of my pulse, hand, hand,

                  fingers, thumb,

my whole body tattooed

              and resounding,

documenting the music

           of my hemispheres,

one of the two sons

          around which

                all this life

          circles.

Sound waves

       do not

       go on

       forever,

          vinyl

            eventually

wears

     itself out, no record

       can truly outlast

            its event,

but that's only

       because ours

           is a system

of hearing that contains

         only

           what it traps,

it's seemingly infinite

         but bounded,

            like

      a drinking glass,

by an eternal brim,

        one that,

          when a lip

dampens it,

      can ring

        to a finger's touch

      seemingly forever,

          over

running
        and endlessly
replenishing.

I.ii

In my core, three others
have entered and turned
each entwining
                    between each,
constantly recentering
                        the shuttle
and, so, binding the selvage
in advance of every sameness
my body will possess.

I don't know what we are but we are
not love, any more than the pieces
of string are the weave—but, like
the string, the crossing over and through
stretches me until love's measuring
says I'm not myself without it.

Outside,
            snow now,
storm in the night, both
premonition
                of the miracle's design
and the design itself,
                        the flakes swirl
                    and seem to tie
            themselves around
each other
            as they streak
                        and spin
        past the streetlight.

When we wake
        in the morning
            to the winter's
                white tapestry,

we rush out and roll
into the blanket,
raise our mittened hands
to cover our cheeks
with the knit
while the vessels
flow red and seem
to braid themselves
together,
flushing at the mere
nearness of
the yarns
we'll spin
around
our beloveds

I.iii

Then there are times when,
                    wildly,
I buck and refuse,
                    turn my eyes
inside my head
            trying
                    to see my mount,
but you
        calmly sit
                    in the saddle
and surely
            don't spare the spurs.

                            Eventually,
I always break
                when I reach the most
plausible
            hypothesis: you
                            cannot be
unseated from me
                    because separation
is a pulp
        Western
                    of my own making,
one that tries
            to whip me
                        like a gallop
            -maddened horse
into the self's
battering pits.

II.i

All that God fuss,
               and then Nietzsche went
and died himself.
               What
a sore winner.

               In the absence
love slips in
               as the devastating
omnipresence,
               that which shimmers
throughout
               the quintessence.
                              So
you stared
          until everywhere
                         you looked you
saw the sun
          for minutes after.

                              So
when I sleep, you seem
                         to trace
onto my eyes
               your absence, wholly
a ghost
          that binds me
                         to you.

                              So
I bend
          to the bathtub to wash
                              your feet,
your hands, your head,
                         I

the disciple,
       you my
              discipline.
Unshriven, I can
              never approach
these visitations
              I purport to call
into language, but
              still you
                     pull me
to the water and wash
                     away any thought
that grace
       must be earned.
                     You draw
with soap
       what seems
              to be the outline
of a holy land
       on your chest, then
rinse it away
       before I can commit it
to memory.
       So
              you remind me
that there is
              the territory
                     and there is
the map,
       and that the territory
is never
       in the map.

II.ii

Hyperspecificity
                    leaves the object
meaningless,
                    too much itself and
too much its type
                    for any definition,
a point played out
                    in the memory
of your terrible
                    twos, a different hue
of a you still so familiar.
                              Chemistry is
the art of discriminating same from
same,
          investigating properties,
                                        how
they combine and change,
                              a clarity
          language sometimes
attempts.
          Which is to say there are
no *et ceteras*
              when we sing,
                              every and each
word,
          sound and gesture
                              means and makes
a difference,
              that speech alone
                                  cannot
express
          the experience
                              of our sleepless
          lunar

                    leaning and rocking
tower
          of babbling song.
                    To search
for what's unique
                    in such an eternal
hymnal
          is trying
                    to see the under
-side of a tattoo
                    while its being beaten
onto your skin.

                    My actual family,
those bodies
                    whose parts
in my speech
                    make a texture
          beyond cognition,
                              losing
          one of you three
                    would be to rip
the lyrics
          from a lullaby.

                    I ask you,
after finding
                    such
                    a glossolalia,
                              how could
even I

          (unable
                    as they say
                              to carry
                    with a bucket
          the tune)

merely *speak*
of this love?

≈≈≈

II.iii

Still, there are days we all
want to pack it in, slough
it away like a snake rubbing
off an irritating skin.
                         Duncan
won't sleep,
             Hugh won't sleep,
and Kelly and I
                 can't.
                         Nerves,
temples, and minds rub and
rage raw. Even the dog looks
sideways as our feet pass by.

We turn to the past to draw
on reserves of fellow-feeling,
but even fracking couldn't find
anything worthwhile in this
hollow earth.
                 It's as though time,
once elapsed, holds no bearing
on the present, as though this
were a dislocated land where
the sky and its stars have to birth
themselves anew every night,
where comets and meteors
scramble the galaxies and
remove the pole star, but we
take these wonders as mere signs.

The love within our love is left
dazed and dumb. We are confused
and refusal becomes our general
condition.
                 If we live outside the world

rather than in it...

     If a sense of dread
turns us towards more extreme and
ever-doomed communities...

       If the disease
that afflicts us leaves behind only increased
knowledge of how easily we're radically
dispossessed of each other...

II.iv

The book open on my desk says that Mao
believed power comes from the barrel
of a gun. That, at least, is a bedrock
stability we can push
                                    away from,
stand up and walk outside.

It is spring, and the sparrows—which Mao
hated—will eat from our hands. We walk
together into the woods knowing we cannot
make the birds come, but we can walk,
and so we walk. The birds are there
or they are not, disbelief in experience
is not an option. We choose to keep
going, and eventually the hugs start
to come, at a charging pace, akimbo,
aslant, athumping, not alighting upon us
but almost pushing through, into us,
sacrament and sacrifice, community,
communion, union. We accept we do not
truly own ourselves, we remember to
disperse, diminish, situate.
                                    We relate,
we relearn to live in relational complexity.
And we are we again. Not blindly optimistic,
but with our hands open and held into the air.

~~~

III.i

The autobiography of the chained
book is one story Middle Ages scribes
never dreamed they were writing.
What's closest at hand is hardest to
—ugh, cliché
        cliché
              cliché
                    that's
what's nearest by, the tale my tired
mind copies out over and over.

So, in the middle of our sleepless
nights, I turn to my books, imagining
nothing could ever be as free—even
the ribbon marking the page seems almost
overwhelmed with choice. Each sits
on its shelf, an iteration of possibility
barely slowed enough for our hand
to reach out and touch it, a shimmering
time leaving behind a time-lapse ghost
of its self that reminds us that the business
of the self is duplication, a ceaseless
dispersion into the words of another,
slipping from the fingers of our lives
and falling into the book that sits there
like an unlocked jewelry box,
a site of secret wealth.

                    Which is where you,
my wee incunabula, record your uncanny
coos, hues, and cries, twin columns
of movable type that I cradle in a hearth-light
that flickers flames on the page that glows
like an underground fire, burning beneath
my forest without ever consuming it,

a scarred and unscathed collection of leaf
falling on leaf. This least vicious of cycles
has bound my life together. So I shape
my book one quire, one young squire
at a time, the signature growing encyclopedic
from D to H, unfolding what
seems to shift by some unknowable means
from folio to quarto, octavo, exponentially
untitled, my two covers, these bookends
of endless means—while I, the grandest
plagiarist, copy the work of these better
young men to scribble my matter. And
watching you, I can imagine a medieval
scriptorium illuminating copies of an obscure
manuscript proposing a general theorem
linking the structure of the human ribcage,
how it expands from the backbone then
folds into itself to snugly contain the vital
organs, to the codex itself, made of skin
and spine, in order to prove writing's
divinity, an argument driving the monks
mad as they write it, a madness adding
further proof to the terrifying power
of written words, until the entire monastery
was burnt to the ground to keep the blasphemy
from spreading, our holiest books, all
buckled and chained, curling their secrets
back into themselves before the ashes
swirl, carrying their words into the wind
where they bury themselves in our over-
whelmed and choking lungs.

III.ii

But a word will not burn,
and so here you are, glowing white hot
in front of me, visitations charging me
with spreading their arcane truths.

So, when I am old and grey, I pray
to remember such books as these
and read again in my cataractic mind
the look in your wordless eyes
as you crawled so boldly up
our Berbered stairs and I
—nearsighted as a star

                              -nosed mole
dazzled out
                of my endarkened
                              hole and
spinning
                high on the terrifying
                                        space
of a world
                opened all
                              around me at once
and flooded
                with light
like a 1976 disco ball,
                                   all
            all and
                           ragdoll spent
—I would recreate these words
as a faith by which to live,
and set about converting the world
to your teachings. But,
as the enraptured Templars
used to say, if you can remember
the Crusades, you weren't really

there at all.

      So my prayers
are that I don't betray you,
my tiny faiths, since I know
that the most devout
too often lose the spirit or,
overwhelmed by sheer fear
of the divine, they lock away
their rosaries and turn
their minds to forgetting
the scriptures.

III.iii

Wait now—
> *when*
> > I'm old and grey?
Well, that 1980s Maurice Richard
Grecian Formula option skated away
so gradually no one noticed long ago,
whether the wife likes it or not.

Then I stand up from the breakfast table
and collect the cereal bowls as my knees'
bands start playing with my hip crunching
along as chorus and you both sing out
"Snap! Crackle! Pop! You're Old!" and
there's no penalty for looking this happy.

III.iv

Sure, we try to step outside ourselves
and study our ugly quirks, those quarks
that scurry to escape back into the mind's
black holes when love's prism threatens
to refract the light of revelation back
onto us,
            but we're so coloured by the self's
Special Theory of Relative Self-importance,
arguing as it does that $Me=Esprit^2$,
            while
the Newtonian physics of the soul
proves that the gravitational constant
of the universe is that nothing is faster
than the speed of light-hearted deflections
away from every subject getting too close
to delivering uncomfortable self-knowledge.

~~~

III.v

Then one day you ask me outright.

Well, every two-bit hack from
the borscht belt to vaudeville
could make a meal out of saying
it's like being Vice
                    President
—just a heartbeat away
from the nuclear codes,
but
        unless something goes horribly
wrong
            it's a lot of making hot
air speeches no one really
hears, then being handed ugly
souvenirs to take back home from yet
another county fair.
                        But I'd say
it's more collateral damage and
accidental instigation:
                            you're either
lost in a podcast on obscure
tv shows from your childhood,
sympathizing with the technical
troubles of shooting Fonzie
over the shark tank, bending
over to pick up the last of winter's
stored doggie-doo from the lawn
when the drive-by's ricochet
hits you square in your favorite
cheek
        or
            it's walking past the doctor's
laboratory and
                    Hey, that door

she always keeps locked is swinging
open, what harm could a quick
look before you get back to plunging
out the toilet possibly cause when
something screams,
                              you spin and
knock
          into the coat rack
                              why
is there a coat rack in a lab
                              you
wonder
          as you watch it rock
                              and topple
next to that button on the wall
marked "Do Not Touch – Monster
Transformation Ray"
                              but
the rack rights itself
                              harmlessly
          and then
you slip on a forgotten bag
of dogpoo that fell from your
pocket in the excitement,
                              whack
your forehead right
                              through the wall
completing
          the inevitable circuit,
                              firing
off the beam at the beautiful young
boy
          who's charging at you, now
like a rabid wolfman, now
Dracula,
          now
                    the monster of Franken
Castle,

just as the voice in your earbuds
reminds you that eventually
the Scooby Gang found out those
were all really disguises of the
same mischievous miscreant,
foiled at last
            not by Fred's carefully
placed net but through the bumbling fool's
simple good luck.
            Yes,
                  I tell you,
fathering's exactly like that.

IV.i

When you hold two things, one familiar and
one foreign, your sum total of knowledge refuses
the balance and recalculates everything. This is clearly
the clearest this point can be stated. You start
to enter the wordable world and its deification
of reality. I watch you invent a conversation
with the absent. You hold your books to your mouth,
and I imagine you licking the words like nectar
from the pages, eating each one like a honeycake
with an alphabet printed on it. You take language
into you, and ingest a love like no other, you
hold all the letters, waiting, on your tongue.

IV.ii

You part your lips and out tumbles small volumes
of devotional proverbs which I try to scribble down
to use as my private matins. It's so damn early,
but you rest in my hands like a wee Book of Hours,
made to be read day after day, week after week,
month after year. A difference surrounds you
—not a claptrap cliché about opposites, but
a difference working away at a world trapped
in a sameness of minds, where our thoughts and
wants run infinitely into themselves like the toy
train on your floor chugging on tracks in figures
of eight, in which only love offers the imperial
necessity of otherness. My hand on your chest
as you lie newly naked on the table, I bend down
and reach for a clean diaper as you spray diarrhea
on the wall just behind me. Like a man miraculously
missed by all the bullets from the firing squad,
I stand there, dazed, dazzled just to be alive.

IV.iii

Because their footprints in the mud resembled
cuneiform writing, birds were believed
by Mesopotamians to transcribe the thoughts
of the gods. Better to mark out the walkways
with barley-meal and watch the songbirds,
fickle little oracles, fly down and feed, scattering
every path into twisted, unreadable sentences.

So go the treatises on love.

This baby is my interpreter of whatever the divine
might say, and he winks and coos when I ask
if a space,
        such as a bookstore,
                ordered by artificial
categories, resonates the existence of a logical universe,
a nursery in which everything has its place,
                  or if all
memories take form only in spaces of chaos, gapped
as shelves of a looted library. If the classical texts
are infallible, what room is there for interpretation?

Abelard himself saw love, like the resort to authority,
as a chain by which beasts are led blindly. Please pull
the chain gently, or take me by the hand and recite the day
as a Bible blasphemously transcribed into contradictory
translations, a never-ending wealth of sacred iterations
where words bridge the gaps between our cells.

IV.iv

To speak in generalities is dangerously
silly, but the poet's heart, so celebrated
in the poet's own song, though rarely
elsewhere, is comparable to a carefully
aimed rifle. As in the old love cults,
there is a string of broken women
and men more fitting to Orwell's image
of the eternal boot than to the tender
blush we all want to imagine. Sappho
described Eros as *lusimeles*, "the loosener
of limbs"—which is delightful,

                                     until
the scholar of Greek explains it's not
a calming relaxant, but rather "a force
so powerful it dissolves the joints
and disjoins the body, disarticulating
the part from the whole," a dismem
-berment or dislocation more disinterment
than a desiring discernment. What is
required is an imaginative transformation
of reality, a freedom of the mind as an act
of survivance, and love is how we pull free
from the drowning hand of habit pushing
down on our necks.

                         You move in your body
with a commingling twist that seeks neither
to submerge your will in a wider process
of world creation, nor to retain an individual
control of meaning. Your squirms seem to say
that love is the possibility without which we are
incomplete. I can only say that it is an ultimate
health, that with it I resist the infection
of purely private events.

V

In the end, not *what* love is but *that* it is,
that's enough. Still, it's an absent site,
one best approached by obscure words
tied to the mysteries of water, it is *benthic*
or *lacustrine*, terms with a dark terror
shimmering in their corners, a rippling
that suggests something, some *thing*
that knows how to disrupt the surface
of the sea without ever relaxing
the imagination by showing itself,
a subliminal coil in the edge of the film's
flickering frame, a negative left
undeveloped—and yet it's the positive
prod to get on with it, to work, be it
earthworks, spadeworks, groundworks.
A loveworks digging in the lake for the day's
lost glow. Logic holds little currency here.
This is the human prayer, what we plead
and barter in silence into our cupped hands
because we cannot pull love, comprehensible
and provable, to exist as an easy proof
for the general public, it flicks like a prehensile
tail near the boat and is gone before the captain
can believe it.
       Working the nets of this accosting
exchange between wonder and belief in a society
of exhausted lovers pushes our minds astray,
we drop our oars and float adrift, spellbound
and confused by what could be causing
the flowing surface's approaching swelling rift.

So, water into air, dark into light, word or other
word, how do we hook and drag such a
an experience from its abyss?

Looking at the lake at night, a child knows
the flat field of reflected lights is a series of depths
of incalculable distances, sets of eyes gleaming
from an underneath where there is no holding
them away, and the strain is etched into the walls
of his brain cells like shapes scratched uncountable
years ago into the stones of a sea cave forgotten
so long ago the crews of the fishing boats sail over it
every day without even shivering, no clue that every
minute love is watching and waiting for the moment
to capsize us.

VI.i

Ah boys, you come trailing white clouds
of masculine glory, a lineage of builders
and founders and makers of glorious
glories, and the glories are glorious,
the beauties are beauteous. But shouldn't
we be more than a little tired of this
spectacular bullshit? Aren't great artists
who are garbage people still garbage?
Or can we throw out just the sexist crybaby
if the bathwater is clean? You can stare
at the magnificent buildings but that
doesn't help what the foundations ploughed
under, the legacy of a rapacious world
too often made by men who looked
a lot like us.

VI.ii

We're looked back on more gently than we deserve,
history loses our stumbling around in the dark, arms
flailing, fumbling, toes constantly bruised and knees
ever bloodied, all for the want, the lack of this nearsense,
the sight, sound, scent, taste, and touch of the whole
body just before us. And what does it do to the world
if some still choose to view such pain as a needed
byproduct of love, runoff, offal, not an opposite
but a waste mold necessary to the casting
of our better selves?
     My god, this is maudlin.
If I have no answers, it's rude trade to leave you
with questions, but here endeth my lesson,
still yammering on and on about white men,
as white men are wont to do.

VII.i

You wiggle in your booster seat,
nothing on but a diaper and a smile,
and announce *apples make me waddle.*
Penguins waddle into the water. Duncan
has picture day and has chosen a crisp,
light blue dress shirt and a sharp, dark
blue tie, over jeans, to *look like a cool*
businessman on a yacht. He's been in grade
one for three whole weeks. Life's rowboat
shifts inside me but today the seas are calm
and love floats in the room like a buoy.

VII.ii

Boys—my great leaps forward—
my whispered rosaries go to you
for the myriad ways I fail, have
failed, and will continue to fail
you. I am such a litany of sins
of commission and omission.
                                Please
understand that this writing man
was always my better self, that
my greatest sin is that I will never
be him, though my greatest win
is that he will never, never articulate
what I feel for you because I know you
as a way of being too complete to ever
piece and parcel into words.
                            And these two
squirming, squirreling, quarreling
bodies never at rest are surely beyond,
in every way, my understanding, and
moments when I think otherwise
are my most mortal error, an immoral
terror, though even then you raise me
in a most fortunate fall, as surely as
the water rises in the sprinkler
                                    only
to not fall, to bead on your bodies,
in your mouth, in your eyes and ears
as you wrap the world
                        like twin stars
bending light and gravity around you,
you giggling pulsars of life.
                        And so I do
learn myself more through you, of you,
with you, you beaming beetles scuttling
into the darkest holes of my self before

becoming fireflies buzzing to set me
aflame like a blazing bush that does
not burn though it kindles a halo
beyond itself, just as some say
there is no such thing as love,
only loving.

VII.iii

If I could, this is where I would
choose to stand, coiled inside
a rhythm of attention sited
at the conflict of time and
the actual world, that, every
day, exposes a puzzle piece
of our world as it fades, like
a film glimpsed as it's pulled
from the camera, the images
dissolving in the sunlight
that shines through the sprinkler
and the skittering squawks
and shocks of its cool water
that blow away in the wind.

VII.iv

As if it were as simple as spinning
on old-time tv dial, regulation tries
to force patterns on us, describing
a circle with a taxonomy that attempts
its never-ending taxidermy.
                                    Luckily,
life is the original soap opera, narratives
end just to force us to further, more glorious
bifurcations and oscillations, we whiplash
from good to bad for no reason at all, and
so there are moments, boys, when you fill me
with so much rage I want to grab the world
by its script, turn to camera and scream
*My God, who writes this shit? Stop fucking
around and figure it out.* Then, cowed like
an aging star miraculously cured from a
contract-dispute-inspired coma, I take
my place in the background, hit my mark,
and channel whatever nonsense I'm told to.
In the end, we're all eventually relegated
to supporting roles in favour of the newest
young talents.
                        And just as cinematographers
working outside, on location, under the ever
-changing position of the sun and the whims
of weather, can look their cocksure directors
in the eye and declare, straight-faced, that
the most unequal and unsteady of all human
dependencies has, is, and always will be
daylight, so character actors like me learn
to stay ready and rely on the largesse
of the real stars.

〜〜〜

VII.v

Marianne, I'm a fan, but
the poem where you discuss
     love—I'm confused why
     you chose to compare
it to a paper nautilus,
     dying for its trust in
     its thin, lonely fortress.

Surely there's something more apt
than this bobbing, not-quite-yet
     fossil to stand in
     for the delicate
concatenations we duet,
     these incantations he
     and I sing to one an

other, a choir chorused out
in the middle of the night?
     Rather than ponder
     the nature of love,
you turn to this lapsed ammonite
     who's more twisted into
     itself than Donne's sonnets.

You stubbornly recuse yourself from
the discussion, twist your
     words like contortion
     -ists spiraling in
to themselves—so your metaphor
     is perfectly convolved.
     So I see that it's me

who's the fool, worrying out
the question like a found shell
     I'm trying to crack

into a straight line
when love's shaped like a carousel,
one that whirls round me, all
ways by always by now.

VIII.i

My little earworms and eye rhymes,
repeated Steinean repetitions of self
and non-self, sensed and nonsensed in
each of my senses, scents synaesthetically
suffused through, within, into,
who permeate, whose permanence
is the immanence in all this
imminence
        —if these words seem
inevitable, it's because the iteration
limits the past's possibility only
to the actual,
        as you two are who
you are, sons and brothers,
and always none of this babble
outside of the I that is hewn
through the we of such us,
        so
we live as pronouns, someone
being something not represented by
but reflected in,
        a memory of what
we're about to see, a plurality of flying
apart at the seems, a speed-reading
of the preceding page as it recedes
into a question of who controls
the proceeding and whose purpose
fluency furthers,
        so not a reaching
back but a passing forth, a lack
that lifts my loving out of the gone,
the zone of things loved, the threat
of the fixed and coherent,
        into the desire
for a pure politics to change my entire

being, where the gaps and angular planes
of the self are collaged together without
comment, the telling juxtapositions
and displacements leftover as I watch you
remake squiggles on the page into words

and so I learn that reading's point
is the pivot joint, the troubled hot spot
from which we're hurled into the world
in meaningful ways to participate in
a culture and lose the solipsism of self,
to sound out forms of liberation in order
to arrive at the duties of the social,
the cursive bonds that tie us together.

VIII.ii

So we twist there, on the tumbling
moebius strip, and we stumble forward,
fall down, and then fall off, somehow fall
up, land again on the tangle and try
to walk over the suspension bridge
as its vectors of tension finally break
free of cohesion and achieve
an adherence to the salvation
of falling.
　　　　　We reach for one another,
the other's open hand the only buoy
in the raging flow, and we grasp as
they clasp us, and we see the boat
that rides the waves is also the boat
that makes waves, we exchange, we
changing our we, we're bound to and
freed by interchange, by connection, not
deciphering, not understanding, there is
no simple except in the complex, so we accept
both and all between, working to welcome
each point of the continuum, all the relays
of the continuance.
　　　　　　　Still, I lie awake
in bed at night, boys, feeling you slip
between my fingers—but then there
you are, next to me, awake and then
asleep, between your mother and me,
linking Kelly to me.

≁≁≁

VIII.iii

But now I've lost the thread
in all this mazing. Perhaps it's less
that you slip between us and more
that you have been teaching me, all
along, to relax these bruised fists into
a community of thumb, index, middle,
ring, little, palm, knuckles, bone, and
the supple, transitory flesh, the right
angles and cuts of shadow and light
that play out an occult cubism, an inter
section of pieces that says every iteration
is a unique reiteration that renews
the matter by straining it between
incarceration, donation, punctuation,
gestation, vexation, elation, filiation,
abdication.

Boys, let's go further, as Monsieur Nancy does.
Love presupposes and proves Thales' point,
all things are filled with gods. It proposes
an unbroken expanse of presence, a world
of continuous truth attaching and stitching
the beloveds to the landscape, makes the actual
a religion flowing through and back to its source,
the mouth, a grand utterance of utterances
so fervent it doesn't allow us a choice
between foment and ferment. It offers us
its one command: reverdure.
                          And in
the billowing tendrils of life's common
divinity, for a moment it's there, the truest
epiphany of the face—hers, his, theirs,
whoever's features force you to care
about the specific
                     —then, that glorious then
of when, now, soon, and forever, you'll care
so much about such and such a face
that you'll see it interlaced in all places,
an ur-face that links us all, what you'll call
the foundation of every face ever suggested.

A satori of love rippling out through all time,
your time, even to my time: as I write this
I feel it as surely as a hand, your hands, your
mother's hand, your lovers' hands, on my hand,
as we draft these lines together. This is the common
wealth.

VIII.v

It's fair to say, much as you
walk to bed carrying the menagerie
of every stuffy you own, it's only
inside our encircled arms that we know,
not just everything, but anything. Always,
we entangle with others or we float free
of ourselves, they're anchors mooring us
to the world, and if I did not have you
I would never have been anything
but a vague dispersal of me, cursed
to wander like a forgotten Greek phantom
away from the sea in search of a place so dry
the people are confused by the oar
on my shoulder.
                        Our odyssey is to go
gather ourselves as part of the world,
to ring the world around us without
fencing ourselves away from it.
                                        So
it's not that the concept of the virtuous
circle doesn't exist but that hugging
—the circuit within the linked hands
and the casual electricity it allows to leap
and loop over and within everything
in its sheltering corral—is its only
example worth speaking of.

∾∾∾

VIII.vi

What arrives in the crossing, crosswise?
Not an accident of being, but being put
into play, neither an environment
nor a neighbourhood. There is no exterior
to objects, there can be no outside.
We speak a mystery of being-in-the-world,
thrown, abandoned, offered, set free.
Sharing.
       This isn't witness but *withness*,
concern *for* as form itself. Love, then,
does not arrive tangled with the affairs
of the world but *is* the tangle, neither
fusion nor discrimination, a single piece
of presence twisted until there is no separation.

It's time to stop all this dithering, the cycles
and recycles, the lather and blather of hithering
and thithering around this unspeakable point:
love *is*, and so the ancient laws of salvage apply,
we keep what we find.

IX.i

All these tumbling words stumbling
after the silences they break, realms
of the possible between incarnate
and immanent, slick tricks somewhere
betwixt the notes and the air music
travels on,
               so we lose
                         ourselves
in the neglects, the derelictions,
the delinquencies, and touch, like
recovery, sounds more plausible
than it turns out to be.
                   We weep
our tears and we weep for others and,
at our best, we weep others' tears and
wash away the language we've horded
inside ourselves through processes
of evaporation, condensation, precipitation,
and let whatever may
                    accumulate by speaking
our catalogues of failures and misdeeds, and
love—not just our desires—exists nowhere
but in the forged links of memory, bands
of neurochemical bonds that mark us both
prisoner and warden.

IX.ii

Still, to say all this is to forget both the return
and the meadow, the everlasting what is,
what that Duncan taught me and what
my Duncan and Hugh, tenderest of pedants,
teach and reteach me: you are as much today
as tomorrow, now as twenty years from now.
The tantrums, the screams and squeals,
the interminable, impossible streams of questions,
challenges, corrections, acceptances are
what you are, now, here, as you serialize
this moment and that, two tangible metaphors
for
    and so,
        and then,
            and yet,
                and
                    and.
Andy's ands, my crushing and running and rum
-maging and rampaging boys, all process and
procedure of holding and enfolding, heaving
anchors by which I tether this
           and this
           and this.

∾∾∾

IX.iii

The dictionary declares the Old English *hewen*
(family, household) obsolete, ties it
to the equally lost *hewe*, a servant
—a whole hidden history of living
together imagined as servitude, beloveds
bound to each other, mastered by one another,
and, sure, we've all been there
                           —but if we jettison
such terms, if language helps us imagine
ourselves to ourselves, how have we let *mastery*
survive since at least 1225? Shouldn't any ties
that bind be left behind? If we eventually erased
the idea that an answering machine was a site
for amateur comedy, surely we can at least try
to resign other problems inherited from the past
with the flick of a pen stroke.
                           If to put something
into
    words requires us to think the unimaginable
outside of words and then cram it into language,
not unlike the plunger trying to stuff matter
down the toilet, what does it mean that we let
ourselves say the shit we say today?
                           But, just as
ambivalence isn't *indifference, anticipation* and
awaiting are radically different, so words carry
legacies as much as meaning, which means we
can reach back and reimagine alternatives:

                                              so,
in the long-lost days, the hewster coloured
the autumn hewt, dunking tired greens
into pots of hewettite, leaves strewn
through slews where the dunkadoos now
gather the tall fescue into the bulrushes
and cattails, folding it all, looping it into a nest,

one whole so obviously made from the complex
fusings of the many, to hold the clutch of eggs,
olive-buff and unspeckled.

                          Language doesn't care
or want us to be better, but that doesn't mean
we shouldn't be.

X.i

The hand is a careless adorant, clueless
and arrogant, mindless in its grasps, its
hasping rasps at the receding world and
like it I sift meaning from this moment in
the way I've been taught to think of the things
in the earth—tombs, silver hordes, and
the fossilized bones of animals long dead
before humans were born—as put there
for us, and so I stand here exhausted and
inexhaustible as that *and*, conjunctively
arrogant enough to try to order the world
and its things, separating them as though
drawing a wire string between every element
of creation, keen enough to cut colour into
pieces, parting kelly green from hunter, fern,
jade, or forest, striating seas into twilight,
midnight, abyssal, as though I could control
benthic terrors as simply as if tracing roads
and maps onto waters could write stop signs
that put an end to the surfacing desires
of the monsters we dream in the deepest
deeps, as though we could think a puzzle
strong enough to baffle the creatures we
imagine into the darkest zones of the mind.

All this and so much unspeakable more
is what I think of as I sit here remembering
taking your hand, fingers around at first,
then inside, then through, and though
medical science assures no transmission
or transfusion could possibly occur to carry
part of you into me, physics and common
sense aren't so sure since I can still feel
the blood in your fingers in mine as you
leaned out from the bank, and we began

to span the river, reaching out over the water,
my countering body weighting us to shore
as the "we" of us was held, suspended,
somewhere in the middle, in the clasp
and clutch of my grasp which was not
as still as the water beneath us, not as fluid
as the water beyond us or as supple
as the water between our legs, not as
carelessly emplaced as the cupola of empty
space between the legs of the heron you
found in the tall grass at the river's bend,
the impetus for all this making and marking
of the blind spot, the essential hiding place
where I look back so intently I finally forget
the looker and even the looking, there is only
fingertips, their nails and their quicks, knuckles
of bones and bend, palm and palm, and locked
between them the space in which we are
and which we are.

X.ii

If the stairs that go up are the same
as those we use to descend, it's by such steps
we take our leave, confused and reaching
for others to guide us. Fozzie Bear guides you
now, though I fear, you, like me, will be led to say
things like *physicality is prior to language*
but language pulls into focus distinctions where
before were only flows of experience, proving
the joke between words and chaos is a complicated
nonequivalence; this world is filled with talk,
yet our beloveds remain neither strictly
empirical nor, as hard as we listen, succinctly
linguistic. It seems unlikely the discourse
of conscience will ever be spoken; however,
later I might obfuscate my befuddlement into
something beyond this bewilderness where all
I do is beg the question to finally appear—but
you're off to bed now, and I'd be remiss if
I didn't tell you, again, the octopuses say
we must pull on our pyjamas, just like
everyone else, four legs at a time. Or as you
eloquently quipped over fistfuls of flying
spaghetti last night, *what the elephants want*
is elephant sunscreen
                              wocka
                   wocka
        wocka

~~~

X.iii

And as I read Neruda writing of the birds
and their "order of the wilds," your eyes
slip before mine like glasses correcting my sight
away from the book to the red-necked grebes
that floated in the breakwater the day before
your third birthday, how first I called them ducks
and you called them ducks, then I called them loons
and you called them loons, and then finally I called
them grebes and you demanded they are, were, will
always be loons. And over your shoulder the tern
fell to the water and tore into its target, a feathered
lance while we crouched behind the benches and hid
from each other, from your brother, from your mother.

Then we climbed onto the rocks and there the mute swan
suddenly at our feet, just feet below, its head plunging
and probing the water, alien and absolutely confusing
to you as it fed and preened, fed and preened, and we
watched the Canada Geese come near and fade away
as the swan stayed just away and the swallows circled
and looped overhead and your hand in mine, my hand
around yours, our hands linked under the swallows,
linked over the swan, linked near the geese, linked
so near to the tern, beyond the grebes that were ducks
and always, yes, always, are loons.

X.iv

Your mother comes with your brother,
their arms linked, and Kelly and I link hands
and we walk, four linked, and we walk, and
we knit together as pieces into one and
separate out into each other as whole parts
of a larger structure, not important in
ourselves but important to ourselves,
to each other, we cleave apart and we
cleave together, we are strands in the tapestry
and we are architecture and arche text,
and we are foundation and abutment,
pile and arch, and we span the entire length
and breadth and story of everything I can
understand as love.

X.v

Strewn and uncanopied, hewing through
life's thickets, still midway upon my journey,
I found the final two paths from which I
do not care to stray, a new trinity, the mother,
the sons, their holy spirits to which I kneel.
Our god is unconditionally granted. But
perhaps it's pointless to philosophize
as though civil factors weren't deeply
at work in how we love: Athenian society
did not see homoeroticism as perverted
or the heteroerotic as normal, but it still
deeply repressed women, pressing them
into the mold of mother, keepers
of the household, and rarely allowed
respectable women on the street.
The social heart, in other words, wants
how it learns to want, and speaking of love
we wade through a river of allusion
that runs hard upon the story underneath
—so, burglars in the night, we try to steal
our salvation as though it were locked away
in a body. And, of course, it is—speech is
prayer, sight and taste are vespers, matins,
and lauds. Touch, the reaching of an arm,
the unfurling of our fingers, is the safety
of what some call the soul. I would quibble
and dodge that point, but I do admit glory
resides in the rising moon of the quick
in the nail of the beloved's little toe, so long
as the lover perceives it: if a god watches
over the little sparrow it is because attention
tends to details in the attended. Ah, this
undulant world, its shifts and flexes pull us
like a wooden, wheeled dog at the end
of a red string into the new, each moment

exploding around us, exploding us, as surely
as I, on my hands and knees, watch over,
minister to, wait upon, frequent, await, and
expect you and follow your flapping footfalls
as though that red string in your hand were tied
through a ring in my nose. As it surely is,
my human bean, my humorous pigeon,
my hue of refracted light shimmering onto
and off the marble statue surrounded in
the square by the water arcing into the pool,
mine because I am incandescently yours.
So I imagine the chisel stroke as it echoes
through the stone mason's arms, one hand holding
the reverberating mallet as each hammer beat
travels from wrist, forearm, upper arm, through
the shoulder and into the trunk of the torso
along sinews and vessels to the body's centre
where it meets, with a shock, the echo
of the stroke that travelled through the chisel's
half of the blow and its half of the mason
as over and over these waves travel their course
to meet in the exact middle of this closed circuit
only to find there an answering pulse echoing
out from the mason's chest, now timed in response
to the movement of arm, hammer, chisel, marble
in an overlapping series of ripples throughout
the body as it sometimes gives itself over to the stone,
sometimes flails itself against it in the seemingly
endless and eternally new action repeated over and
second and second after over, minute to minute,
hour to hour, day in and month out for years,
for lifetimes, as the mason slowly shapes the marble
that slowly shapes his body while the city's fountain
emerges from rock, pouring into and out of
the mason's work and the marble's reply,
so you imagine me as you continue to create
me. The beloved is the messenger but also
the message.

But there is a point in every event
that we cannot see through, and another we
cannot see at all. Love's opacity, then, is its essence.
Which is to say that the peculiar fate of the lover
may be that the most serious questions can only
be posed in the vocabulary of love.
        And I've written
myself into a corner, a full stop, an unproductive
bafflement that freezes my hands over the keyboard,
trying to parse out the difference between hiding
and lying in wait—until there you are, stamping
into my room trailing giggles of glory, grabbing
my hand and pulling me from my seat and this
cerebral dead end, my lovely gosling, my godling,
my Hugh ex machina.

Notes

This project started shortly after the birth of Duncan, when Kelly asked me what I'm sure she meant as a passing question: "Are you going to write something for our son?" Although he had been foremost in my mind for nine months before his arrival, and although he was almost literally all I wanted to think about for months after he arrived, I hadn't thought about writing about him—my previous work hadn't really been *about* anything, and certainly not *about anyone*. I grew to like the idea, but I didn't know how to write a love poem anymore, mostly because I had been trying to write myself out of my writing as much as possible. So, how to write about him without writing about me? It was impossible—but I still wanted to avoid myself as much as possible and so I turned to a process of reading-writing, a way of responding to or challenging existing texts. Over the next few years, I folded my reading indirectly into my writing. My only rule was that I couldn't respond to poetry – poetics, philosophy, novels, etc., were all fair game, but it felt a bit like cheating to adapt poetry into poetry. There are exceptions, but I've directly named those texts or poets, or else I've trusted them to be fairly obvious allusions (as with Eliot and Pound). As the project evolved, nearly all of this reading-writing faded into the background, as multiple drafts caused the poems to take on lives of their own, writing out passages directly responding to others until those texts become more like buried streams running underneath the poem.

When Hugh arrived three years after Duncan, I realized that the project should have two natural halves, one addressed to each of my children. I also thought that, as the third member of my household, Kelly Laycock would be a third part of the project, but I found any attempt to move away from parental love and towards spousal love to be awkward and, to be honest, a bit creepy, given the primary focus. So, while Kelly appears here only in passing, she remains—as in life—the bedrock of the entire enterprise, the only reason the project/family/household exists. I hope that it makes sense to say that I think some loves remain both too close and too large to write about, even in a book focusing on love; that is the case for me with Kelly.

The preamble poem "When I had journeyed half my life's way" references Dante's *Divine Comedy*, Foreigner's "I Want to Know What Love Is," Plato's *Symposium*, Haddaway's "What is Love," and A. E. Housman's "Terence, This is Stupid Stuff."

"Cleave 0.0000" references Wallace Stevens's "Anecdote of the Jar" and the last line of F. Scott Fitzgerald's *The Great Gatsby*.

The ending of "Cleave I.iii" references George Oppen's "Of Being Numerous."

"Cleave II.iii" references the refrain from François Villon's "Ballade des dames du temps jadis" ("Ballad of the Ladies of Bygone Times"), usually translated into English as "But where are the snows of yesteryear?"

"Cleave III.i" adapts the phrase "my skittery pigeon" from Theodore Roethke's "Elegy for Jane."

"Cleave IV.ii" elegizes my friend and colleague Priscila Uppal.

"Cleave V.iii" references Boney M's "Daddy Cool" and Jacques Attali's *Noise*. The latter is a scaffolding text underneath many of the following poems in "Cleave" and "The Bridge."

"ligament / ligature" quotes from A. R. Ammons's *Garbage* (section 16) and references Charles Olson's "*Added to making a Republic in gloom on Watchhouse Point" from *The Maximus Poems: Volume Three*.

"The Bridge I.i" references Dead or Alive's "You Spin Me Round (Like a Record)," The Buggles's "Video Killed the Radio Star," Queen's "Radio ga ga," and Al Perkins's *Hand, Hand, Fingers, Thumb*.

"The Bridge IV.iv" references George Orwell's *1984* ("If you want a picture of the future, imagine a boot stamping on a human face— forever") and quotes from Yopie Prins's *Victorian Sappho*.

"The Bridge VI.i" adjusts Wordsworth's phrase "But trailing clouds of glory do we come" from his "Ode: Intimations of Immortality."

"The Bridge VII.v" takes its inspiration from Marianne Moore's "The Paper Nautilus" and mimics its precise structure (including the odd break from the pattern in the first two lines of the fourth stanza).

"The Bridge VIII.iv" references Jean-Luc Nancy's "Myth Interrupted" from *The Inoperative Community*, in which he works through Thales's "*panta plērē theōn*" ("all things are filled with gods").

"The Bridge VIII.v" references Tiresias's prophecy from Book Eleven of *The Odyssey*.

"The Bridge IX.ii" references Robert Duncan's "Often I Am Permitted to Return to a Meadow."

"The Bridge X.iii" references "The Birds Arrive" from Pablo Neruda's *Canto General* (trans. Jack Schmitt).

This is a list, as best as I can construct it, of the relevant texts I was reading while I wrote *The Loom*. Although they don't appear directly in the poems, many prompted images, thoughts, or starting points for my poems.

Ades, Dawn, editor. *The Dada Reader: A Critical Anthology*. U of Chicago P, 2006.

Alfred, Taiaiake. *Peace, Power, Righteousness: An Indigenous Manifesto*. 2nd ed., Oxford UP, 2009.

Alighieri, Dante. *The Divine Comedy*. Translated by Allen Mandelbaum, Knopf, 1995.

Ammons, A. R. *Garbage: A Poem*. W. W. Norton, 1993.

Attali, Jacques. *Noise: The Political Economy of Music*. Translated by Brian Massumi, Foreword by Fredric Jameson, Afterward by Susan McClary, U of Minnesota P, 1985.

Andrews, Bruce. *Paradise and Method: Poetry and Praxis*. Northwestern UP, 1996.

Bernstein, Charles. *A Poetics*. Harvard UP, 1992.

Billitteri, Carla. *Language and the Renewal of Society in Walt Whitman, Laura (Riding) Jackson, and Charles Olson: The American Cratylus*. Palgrave Macmillan, 2009.

Blanchot, Maurice. *The Unavowable Community*. Introduction and translated by Pierre Joris, Station Hill, 1988.

Broadbent, Laura. *In On the Great Joke*. Coach House, 2016.

Carson, Anne. *Eros the Bittersweet*. Dalkey Archive P, 1998.

Cook, Albert. *Forces in Modern and Postmodern Poetry*. Edited by Peter Baker, Peter Lang, 2008.

Devisch, Ignaas. *Jean-Luc Nancy and the Question of Truth*. Bloomsbury, 2012.

Dewey, Anne Day. *Beyond Maximus: The Construction of Public Voice in Black Mountain Poetry*. Stanford UP, 2007.

Dillard, Annie. *The Writing Life*. Harper Perennial, 2013.

D S H [Dom Sylvester Houédard]. *Notes from the Cosmic Typewriter: The Life and Work of Dom Sylvester Houédard*. Edited by Nicola Simpson. Occasional Papers, 2012.

Duncan, Robert. *The H. D. Book*. Edited and with an introduction by Michael Boughn and Victor Coleman, U of California P, 2011.

Duncan, Robert. *A Selected Prose*. Edited by Robert J. Bertholf, New Directions, 1995.

Dworkin, Craig. *Reading the Illegible*. Northwestern UP, 2003.

Eliot, T. S. "Little Gidding." *The Poems of T. S. Eliot, Volume 1: Collected and Uncollected Poems*. Edited by Christopher Ricks and Jim McCue, Farrar, Straus and Giroux, 2015, pp. 201-209.

Eustis, Helen. *The Horizontal Man. Women Crime Writers: Four Suspense Novels of the 1940s*. Edited by Sarah Weinman. Library of America, pp. 187-392.

Finlay, Ian Hamilton. *Selections*. Edited and with an introduction by Alec Finlay. U of California P, 2012.

Fisher, M. F. K. *Consider the Oyster*. North Point, 1988.

Foucault, Michel. *The Order of Things*. Routledge, 2002.

Fredman, Stephen. *A Menorah for Athena: Charles Reznikoff and the Jewish dilemmas of objectivist poetry*. U of Chicago P, 2001.

Gaiman, Neil. *The Books of Magic*. Illustrated by John Bolton, Scott Hampton, Charles Vess, and Paul Johnson. Introduction by Roger Zelazny. DC Comics, 2014.

Gelpi, Albert, and Robert J. Bertholf, editors. *Robert Duncan and Denise Levertov: The Poetry of Politics, the Politics of Poetry*. Stanford UP, 2006.

González Echevarría, Roberto. "Neruda's *Canto General*, The Poetics of Betrayal." Introduction. Pablo Neruda, *Canto General*, translated by Jack Schmitt, U of California P, 1991, pp. 1-12.

Hagy, Alyson. *Scribe*. Graywolf, 2018.

Hejinian, Lyn. *My Life and My Life in the Nineties*. Wesleyan UP, 2013.

———. *The Language of Inquiry*. U of California P, 2000.

Hochman, Hugh. "Where Poetry Points: Deixis and Poetry's 'You' in Eluard and Desnos." *French Studies*, vol. 59, no. 2, 2005, pp. 173-88.

Kim, Myung Mi. "Pollen Fossil Record." *Commons*, U of California P, 2002.

Levertov, Denise. "Some Notes on Organic Form." *Postmodern American Poetry: A Norton Anthology*, edited by Paul Hoover, W. W. Norton, 1994, pp. 628-33.

Macdonald, Helen. *H is for Hawk*. Hamish Hamilton, 2014.

Manguel, Alberto. *A History of Reading*. Vintage Canada, 1996.

Marlatt, Daphne. *Ana Historic*. House of Anansi P, 1997.

Mayer, Bernadette. "Author's Note" [*Sonnets*]. *Tender Omnibus: The First 25 Years of Tender Buttons Press 1989-2014*, edited by Katy Bohinc, Tender Buttons, 2016, p. 85.

Moore, Marianne. "The Paper Nautilus." *New Collected Poems*, edited by Heather Cass White, Farrar, Straus and Giroux, 2017, p. 158

Moten, Fred. *The Little Edges*. Wesleyan UP, 2015.

Moure, Erín. "Fidelity Was Never My Aim (But Felicity)." *My Beloved Wager: Essays from a Writing Practice*, NeWest P, 2009, pp. 187-194.

Marie-Eve Morin, *Jean-Luc Nancy*. Polity, 2012.

Nancy, Jean-Luc. *Being Singular Plural*. Translated by Robert D. Richardson and Anne E. O'Byrne, Stanford UP, 2000.

———. *The Inoperative Community*. Translated by Peter Connor, Lisa Garbus, Michael Holland, and Simona Sawhney, U of Minnesota P, 1991.

———. *On the Commerce of Thinking: of Books and Bookstores*. Translated by David Wills, Fordham UP, 2009.

Nichol, bp. *Truth: A Book of Fictions*. Edited by Irene Niechoda, Mercury, 1993.

Nichols, Miriam. *Radical Affections: Essays on the Poetics of Outside*. U of Alabama P, 2010.

Olson, Charles. "*Added to / making a Republic." *The Maximus Poems*, edited by George F. Butterick, U of California P, 1983, p. 584.

Olson, Charles, and Robert Creeley. *Charles Olson & Robert Creeley: The Complete Correspondence*. Edited by George Butterick. Vol. 4. Black Sparrow, 1982.

Petrosky, Henry. *The Book on the Bookshelf*. Vintage, 1999.

Plato. *Symposium*. Translated by Robin Waterfield. Oxford UP, 1994.

Prins, Yopie. *Victorian Sappho*. Princeton UP, 1999.

Redding, Arthur. *Radical Legacies: Twentieth-Century Public Intellectuals in the United States*. Lexington, 2016.

Rich, Adrienne. "When We Dead Awaken: Writing as Re-Vision." *Essential Essays: Culture, Politics, and the Art of Poetry*, edited by Sandra M. Gilbert, W. W. Norton, 2018, pp. 3-19.

Smith, Patti. *Just Kids*. Ecco, 2010.

Stein, Gertrude. "*from* A Transatlantic Interview." *The Norton Anthology of Modern and Contemporary Poetry*, edited by Jahan Ramazani et al. 3rd ed., vol. 1, W. W. Norton, 2003, pp. 986-93.

Stewart, Susan. *Poetry and the Fate of the Senses*. U of Chicago P, 2002.

Swift, Daniel. *The Bughouse: The Poetry, Politics, and Madness of Ezra Pound*. Farrar, Straus and Giroux, 2017.

Woolf, Virginia. *Mrs. Dalloway*. Edited by David Bradshaw, Oxford UP, 2000.

Acknowledgements

I would like to thank Dani Spinosa and Kate Siklosi for their friendship and support; they not only published an earlier, smaller version of this project as the chapbook *Haecceity* for their Gap Riot Press, but they also provided valuable comments, as did Adam Dickinson and Stephen Cain, on the completed manuscript. rob mclennan published several sections, in earlier forms, through his above/ground chapbook press, and also recommended my work to Ryan Fitzpatrick, who published "Ligament / Ligature" as an online chapbook through his Model Press. The late and much missed Robert Hogg included several sections in an issue of *The Café Review* on Canadian poetry that he guest edited. Sections from the poem also appeared in *Untethered*, *The Angle*, *fillingStation*, *Prairie Fire*, *Grain*, *Touch the Donkey*, and as a Happy Monks broadside. My sincerest thanks and love to each of the editors and friends involved in these publications.

I would also like to thank everyone at the University of Calgary Press. Starting with the two anonymous reviewers (both of whom offered very helpful suggestions), everyone at the press has worked to improve this book. I would especially like to thank my editor, Helen Hajnoczky. Helen provided superb, insightful editing that clarified and refocused these poems in a profoundly subtle and extremely deft manner. Her work managed to not only improve the poems, but to make them more accurately what I wanted them to be. I am profoundly grateful to her.

Kelly Laycock was the first and best sounding board for all the pieces in this collection. She gently prodded and pulled me into areas that I was, at first, not sure about, but I eventually came to see them as best and necessary. As in day-to-day actuality, Kelly has made everything here much better than I could ever have made it by myself.

My mind holds times together
like a man holding still two horses
running in opposite directions:
           —your mother is six months along,
                growing our new world.
My lines swell, too, the brim trembles yet
somehow holds and then still holds more.

        —my hand leaves the back of your bicycle seat
            and leaves the back of your brother's.
Years later I write that road in my mind daily
and hear your squeals of success still
hanging like cocoons and beehives in the trees.

        —school and first feedings, long nights
            and fevers, short days and screaming
            Scooby Doo flights of fantasy, what
horrors would I have gotten away with
without these meddling kids?
I dig memories into the earth and
like a greedy Great Dane dig them all up
again and again.
                    But what remains
buried shifts and changes structure
without my even knowing.
                        Ah, boys,
this is my poorly trestled walk
over the colliery of my too-human desire.
And still, still, *I comed to see you,*
you said, *I runned down the stairs,*
the world was all tilty and perfect.

        —and now I jump from the bathtub
        finally understanding the volume
        of love, the irregular shape that leaves
        each of us running naked through the streets
        for all to see, yelling *I have it! I have it!*

Perhaps this is not all we know on earth,
or all we need to know of love or its strange,
estranged alchemies, but it is how the song,
at least for the moment, extends
                    attends
                    amends

ANDY WEAVER is a settler writer and scholar. He is an associate professor of creative writing, contemporary poetry, and poetics at York University in Toronto and author of the poetry collections *Were the Bees, Gangson,* and *This.*

BRAVE & BRILLIANT SERIES

SERIES EDITOR: Aritha van Herk, Professor, English, University of Calgary
ISSN 2371-7238 (PRINT) ISSN 2371-7246 (ONLINE)